Young Americans

Tales of Teenage Immigrants

John DiConsiglio

SCHOLASTIC INC.
New York Toronto London Auckland Sydney
Mexico City New Delhi Hong Kong Buenos Aires

4230500203457

Cover photo
Mary Gow © Scholastic Inc.

Adapted from *Coming to America: Voices of Teenage Immigrants* by John DiConsiglio.
Copyright © 2002 by Scholastic Inc. Published by Scholastic Inc. All rights reserved.

No part of this publication may be reproduced in whole or in part, or stored in a retrieval system, or transmitted in any form or by any means, electronic, mechanical, photocopying, recording, or otherwise, without written permission of the publisher. For information regarding permission, write to Scholastic Inc., 557 Broadway, New York, NY 10012.

Copyright © 2005 by Scholastic Inc.
All rights reserved. Published by Scholastic Inc.
Printed in the U.S.A.

ISBN 0-439-12405-0
(meets NASTA specifications)

SCHOLASTIC, READ 180, and associated logos and designs are trademarks and/or registered trademarks of Scholastic Inc.

LEXILE is a registered trademark of MetaMetrics, Inc.

4   5   6   7   8   9   10   23   13 12 11 10 09 08 07 06

Contents

Introduction

"America can be very hard," says Alexis Aguirre. He's 15. He came to the United States from El Salvador.

Alexis explains, "You are in a new world. You work and work and work. You have to learn a new language. You have to fit in with new kids. But once you get here, you can be anything you want."

Every year, nearly 9 million **immigrants** come to the United States. Many of them are teenagers like Alexis. These kids have left their friends and homes. Many ran away from **poverty** and war.

Most come to the United States with a

dream. They want freedom. They want to work hard. And they want to live better than they did before.

Here are the stories of four teenage immigrants. Some are doing great in the U.S. Some are having a hard time.

The U.S. has been called a **nation** of immigrants. This is their story.

The World

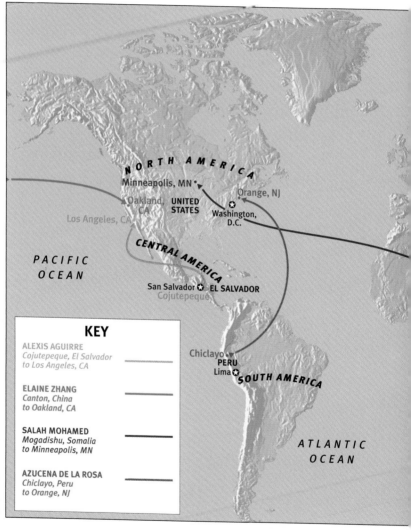

NORTH AMERICA

Minneapolis, MN

Orange, NJ

Oakland, CA UNITED STATES

Washington, D.C.

Los Angeles, CA

PACIFIC OCEAN

CENTRAL AMERICA

San Salvador ✪ EL SALVADOR
Cojutepeque

Chiclayo
PERU
Lima ✪ SOUTH AMERICA

ATLANTIC OCEAN

KEY

ALEXIS AGUIRRE
Cojutepeque, El Salvador to Los Angeles, CA

ELAINE ZHANG
Canton, China to Oakland, CA

SALAH MOHAMED
Mogadishu, Somalia to Minneapolis, MN

AZUCENA DE LA ROSA
Chiclayo, Peru to Orange, NJ

Carol Zuber-Mallison

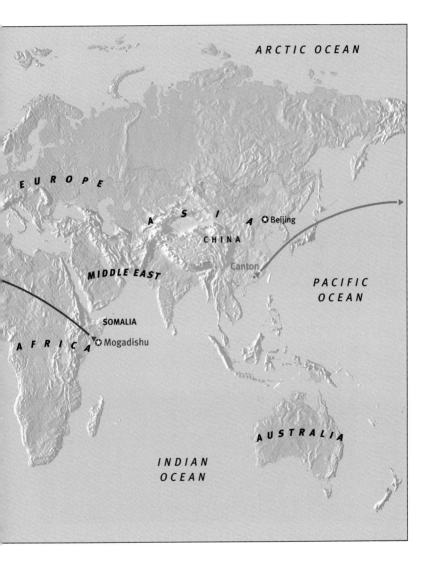

Mary Gow © Scholastic Inc.

When Alexis was seven years old, he left El Salvador to join his parents in Los Angeles. It took him 12 days to reach the U.S.

"The first night in Los Angeles, my heart was racing. It was like an adventure about to begin."

Alexis Otoniel Aguirre

El Salvador

Alexis was young when he left El Salvador. He was seven years old. His family didn't have much money. But they wanted to come to the United States. They saved for four years. Still, they had to leave one at a time.

First, Alexis's father went. He settled in Los Angeles. He wrote letters home and sent money. Alexis was five at the time. A year later, Alexis's mother left. Then, his younger brother was gone. Alexis was left alone with his grandparents.

When it was finally time to leave, Alexis cried. He didn't want to leave his grandparents. His grandmother gave him ten dollars. His grandfather placed a religious medal in his hand. "It's for you, Alexis," his grandfather said. Then he wiped his grandson's tears away. "It's for good luck and protection in the new world."

For 12 days, Alexis traveled north. He took buses through Guatemala. He rode in a truck through Mexico. Friends of his mother took care of him. Alexis didn't speak much. He held his grandfather's medal tightly. And he wondered where on earth he was going. "I didn't know if I was excited or scared," he says.

Alexis was only seven. But he was leaving his whole life behind.

Alexis was born in the tiny village of El Espinal. Only about 1,000 people lived there. Everyone grew their own food. The whole town shared a **community** garden. People would gather there and share fruits

Alexis sits with his brother and parents in their home in Los Angeles. In the U.S., Alexis's parents have to work very hard. "But our family is together, so we are happy," he says.

and vegetables. "Those gardens are the happiest memory of my **homeland**," Alexis says.

Other memories aren't so happy. Most people in El Espinal were very poor. Huge families lived in small houses. Fifteen people might sleep in a single bedroom. Roads were not paved. Rain turned the streets into big mud puddles.

Alexis walked three miles to school every day. The school was just a single room. Kids of all ages were packed inside. The school had a band. But the drums were made of cans. The **cymbals** were tin pie plates.

Alexis's father wasn't around much. He drank a lot. Sometimes neighbors saw him on the street. They would tell Alexis's mother about it. "I saw your husband passed out last night," they would say. But when he was home, Alexis's father was good to the kids. "He loved us a lot," says Alexis.

At the time, a **civil war** was tearing El Salvador apart. Alexis remembers planes dropping bombs at night. His mother would put him under the bed for safety.

Some nights, his mother would sit next to him. "Life will be better in the United States," she would say. "If you work hard, you can be anything you want."

Finally, Alexis was about to find out what the United States was really like. He arrived in Los Angeles. He was still holding his grandfather's medal. He was nervous.

"I didn't know what to think about my father," Alexis says. "I didn't remember him at all. I wasn't sure I knew what he looked like."

Alexis's father had stopped drinking. He had gotten a job as a painter. And Alexis recognized him right away. "I remember running to him and hugging him tight," says Alexis. "I didn't let go of him for a very long time."

That night, Alexis took a bath in hot water for the first time. Later, the whole family crowded into one bed. Alexis was too excited to sleep. "My heart was racing," he says. "It was like an adventure about to begin."

The next day, his father bought him shoes. Alexis had been wearing his grandfather's shoes. They were four sizes too big.

The day after that, Alexis went to school. He spoke almost no English. But he

Mary Gow © Scholastic Inc.

Alexis stands near the famous Hollywood sign in Los Angeles. He has learned English and does well in school. Alexis says, "Already I have achieved some of what you would call the American dream."

sat in class and listened. Before long, he spoke perfectly.

Now, there's one thing Alexis loves about the United States. He loves the **diversity**. "I have friends who are Hispanic, Korean, white, black," he says. "You can't just say, 'I will only be friends with Central Americans.' Or, 'I will not talk to immigrants.' You have to talk to everyone."

The Aguirres are still very poor. Alexis's father often works 15 hours a day.

But Alexis thinks his mother was right about the United States. His life will be better. Alexis's mother quit school after sixth grade. His dad didn't get past ninth grade. Alexis is already in tenth grade.

"I want to have a better life than they did," Alexis says. "That's why they brought me here. And that's why they work so hard. And if I ever have kids, I want them to have a better life than me."

Do you think Alexis will have a better life than his parents? Why or why not?

Elaine Zhang says she's torn between two worlds: China and the United States. "I try to think of myself as an American," she explains. "But I cannot forget China."

Mary Gow © Scholastic Inc.

"My parents gave up everything to bring me here. I cannot let them down."

Elaine Zhang

China

In China, Elaine Zhang lived in a five-room house. She played in a big backyard. Her family had two cars. Her father owned a restaurant.

Elaine and her mother were close. They went shopping together. They talked about Elaine's boyfriends and school. "In China, she loved me a lot," Elaine says. "She really loved me. Not like now."

Now, in the United States, everything has changed. There isn't much money. Elaine's father has no job. Her mother works at a supermarket.

At night, Elaine's mother comes home unhappy. Elaine might be watching TV or reading. Sometimes she's on the phone with friends. And her mother gets mad.

"She yells at me because I am not studying," Elaine says. "She yells at me because I am not cooking or doing the laundry. She yells at me because I do not have many American friends."

Elaine doesn't know what she did wrong. Often, she starts crying. "Are you my mom?" she asks. "I don't feel like I am your kid anymore."

Sometimes, Elaine just wants to go back to China. "I wish we never came here," she says.

Elaine remembers China well. She says she was happy in Canton, a city in southeast China. She didn't worry much. She hung out with friends. They went to **karaoke**. They talked about boyfriends.

But Elaine also knows there were problems. Her great-great-grandparents had been rich business owners in China.

Then the **Communists** won a civil war. They took over the government. They took money from rich people. Elaine's great-great-grandparents lost their home and their business. They were forced to work on a farm.

Today, Elaine wouldn't be forced into a job. But many Chinese girls still don't have lots of choices. Most don't get past eighth grade. Very few go to college. Elaine's parents wanted more for their daughter.

So, they decided to come to the United States. They left China when Elaine was 13. They settled in Oakland, California.

Right away, the Zhangs wanted their daughter to act American. In China, her name had been Shu Ling. They told her it was now Elaine. "Only speak English at home," they said. "Only date American boys. You are in America now. Forget China."

Elaine didn't understand. She hated her

"My parents wanted me to choose what I could do with my life," Elaine, 20, says. "In China, girls have fewer choices. Most have less than an eighth-grade education."

new home. The family lived in a tiny apartment. It only had two rooms. Elaine and her sister shared a bed. Even the food seemed strange to her. In China, she ate rice all the time. In Oakland, she ate hamburgers, pizza, and french fries. Before long, she gained 30 pounds.

School was especially tough. "I had to learn everything over again, like a baby," she says. "My ABCs. My 1-2-3s."

At first, kids made fun of her. They called her names. They said mean things. "Go back to China," they would say.

Then, Elaine started to speak better English. The Americans seemed friendlier to her. "In China, there is much competition," she says. "Other kids will not help you. Here kids help each other all the time."

Now, Elaine has some American friends. They want to go to karaoke with her. "You are 18 now," they say. "You need to have fun." She's gotten flowers from American guys. They want to date her.

But Elaine usually says no. She has no time for fun. She has to study. "My parents gave up everything to bring me here," she says. "I cannot let them down."

Elaine still disagrees with her parents. They want her to be a doctor. But Elaine hates biology. She wants to be a teacher.

Her mother argues with her. "A teacher

Elaine *(center)* works as a volunteer. She helps female immigrants from Asia. The women need help learning how to live in the U.S.

doesn't make money," she yells. "A doctor makes money." She wants Elaine to get a better job. She wants her to live in a nicer place. She wants her to fit in.

Elaine tries to understand her mother. "She works so hard," Elaine says. "Her boss yells at her. She comes home so tired. There is nothing she can change about that. The only thing she can change is me."

So, Elaine tries to change. She's learned

to speak English. She's made American friends. And she tries to think of herself as American.

Elaine thinks it's good that she is trying to fit in. She is much happier. But still, there's something missing. "Have you ever been hurt?" she asks. "You get better. But sometimes you have scars. I have many scars on my heart."

Do you think Elaine's parents made the right choice by coming to America? Why or why not?

Salah Mohamed is from Mogadishu, Somalia. When he was 10 years old, heavy fighting broke out. "Every day I would hear missiles and gunshots," he remembers.

© Bruce Kluckhohn/Getty Images for Scholastic Inc.

"I am Somali, and I am Muslim. But I live in America. And I love it here."

Salah Mohamed

Somalia

Salah Mohamed is a long way from home. He lives in Rochester, Minnesota. He was born in Mogadishu, Somalia. "It's a different world from here," he says.

That's a problem for Somali kids in the United States. "They have to make a choice," says Salah. "Are they going to be Somali? Or are they going to be American?"

Some kids make the switch. They wear American clothes. They date American kids. They stop their **Muslim** prayers. They forget their traditions.

Others try not to change at all. They have only Somali friends. They don't listen to American music. They never go to parties.

Where does Salah fit in? He's not sure. He moved here in 2000. He still feels like a Somali. But he likes watching Americans. "I like the way they talk and laugh," he says. "They have so much freedom and **confidence**."

Salah hasn't told his mother this. She wants him to stay Somali. "But in many ways," he says, "I want to be just like the Americans."

Salah remembers a lot about Somalia. Most people there are Muslim. In Mogadishu, every block had a **mosque**. People prayed five times a day. Each time, a man sang from a window in a mosque. He was calling people to prayers. "I really miss hearing that," Salah says.

Salah's father was a religious leader. He was also a **merchant**. The family had plenty of money. They lived well.

Then the civil war came. Salah was ten when it started. The whole family was

© Bruce Kluckhohn/Getty Images for Scholastic Inc.

Salah and his mother, Sadia, at their home in Rochester, Minnesota. Sadia was in the United States two years before she could send for her kids. "She wrote every day," Salah says.

scared. They heard gunshots and missiles every day. Who would be the next one to die?

In weeks, the city was destroyed. Businesses were gone. Roads were ruined. "Everything was wiped out," Salah says.

The family made plans to leave. But **rebels** captured and killed Salah's father. The family never got to see the body.

The next year, Salah and his family finally got out. They went to Kenya, in east Africa. They settled in a **refugee** camp, a place for people without homes. Salah hated it there. People were crowded into tiny tents. There wasn't enough food. People were always getting sick.

Salah heard everyone in the camp talk about the United States. The schools were good, they said. Americans were supposed to be friendly. Everyone was rich. People said there was money just lying in the street.

Salah's mother, Sadia, asked to be allowed into the United States. It took five years, but the U.S. government finally said yes. Sadia had a sister in Minneapolis. The sister got her a job. And in 1998, Sadia went to the United States. Salah stayed behind with his sister and three brothers.

Sadia saved money. She wrote to her kids every day. In two years, they were able to join her.

Salah, 19, in the traditional Somali robe, called a *kamis*. He wears it on Fridays, the Muslim holy day. He also wears it on other important Muslim holidays.

© Bruce Kluckhohn/Getty Images for Scholastic Inc.

© Bruce Kluckhohn/Getty Images for Scholastic Inc.

Salah and his family stand outside their home. Left to right: Salah's brother, Mohamed, 13; his cousin, Mohamed Isse, 14; his mother, Sadia; his brother, Abdell, 8; and his sister, Sosia, 11.

Finally, Salah had made it to the United States. But fitting in wasn't easy. Kids at school made fun of him. They mocked the way he spoke. They teased him about his clothes. Friday is a holy day for Muslims. Salah would wear a Somali robe to school. It's called a *kamis*. "Why are you wearing a dress?" kids would say.

"I was depressed at first," Salah says.

But a teacher helped him out. She said the other kids just didn't understand. So, Salah tried to teach them. They'd ask about his *kamis*. He'd tell them about his religion. They'd ask why he sometimes left class early. He'd tell them he went to pray.

Before long, Salah made friends. He's still amazed by American kids. "American kids in school have fun," he says. "They talk back to their teachers. They joke and laugh out loud." In Somalia, kids never talked in school. They'd be whipped if they did.

One day, Salah made a joke in class. He waited for the teacher to get mad. But everyone laughed. "I could barely stop smiling," Salah says.

American kids are amazing in another way to Salah. They date. They hold hands in the hallway. They kiss in public. "That doesn't happen with us," Salah says. It's against his religion.

"I have never dated an American girl,"

Salah says. "It would be strange. And it would upset my mother. But American girls are so filled with life."

So, Salah still hasn't made the choice. He may never really choose. "I am Somali, and I am Muslim," he says. "But I live in America. And I love it here."

How would you feel if you had to move to another country?

"I want to sit in a classroom with other students and talk about books or science or psychology. That's my American dream."

Azucena De La Rosa

Peru

Azucena sat in a field in Mexico. She was five years old. A helicopter zoomed over her head. It searched the ground with bright lights. She ducked low in the tall grass. She sat with her mother, her aunt, and her cousin. And she hugged a small doll. It was the only thing left of her life in Peru.

Across the field lay California. If they made it, Azucena would meet another aunt. They would fly to New Jersey. And they would start a new life in the United States.

First, they had to get past the helicopters. The helicopters carried **border** police. The police were looking for **illegal** immigrants.

© Bradley Olman/Olman Photo for Scholastic Inc.

Azucena lived in the United States for 15 years before she received a **green card**. Until then there were many **privileges** she couldn't enjoy—like getting money for college.

But the De La Rosas had help. They had paid a man $1,500. It was almost all the money they had. But they thought it was worth it. The man was a Coyote. Coyotes help people sneak across the border.

The helicopters flew past again. The Coyote yelled, "Run!" He grabbed one of Azucena's hands. Her mother grabbed the other. They lifted her and started running.

Azucena saw city lights ahead. It was San Diego. They ran and ran and ran. The city never seemed to get closer. "It seemed like it was impossible," she remembers. "We'd never reach those lights."

But they made it. Azucena's aunt was waiting. They flew to New Jersey. And Azucena began her new life.

Azucena has been in the United States since 1986. But she lived in the country illegally. "I was an illegal **alien**," she says. She and her mother didn't have permission from the U.S. government to live here.

Illegal aliens like Azucena are allowed to go to school. But it's not legal for them to have jobs.

Most of the time, Azucena says, it didn't matter that she was an illegal alien. She liked school and got good grades. She was popular. She had American friends and **Latino** friends. Most kids didn't even know that she was illegal.

Azucena was also making plans for the future. She wanted to go to college. And she wanted to become a **psychologist**.

In Peru, Azucena says, she wouldn't have that chance. Most of the schools aren't very good. And most girls don't get good educations. Could she be a psychologist in Peru? Azucena doesn't think so. "They would laugh at me," she says. "They would tell me to find a husband."

Still, life in the U.S. had its problems. Once, Azucena got a job at a clothing store. She gave the manager a fake name. And she made up a **social security number**.

For a while, everything was fine. Then the store hired a new girl. She was from Azucena's school. "She turned me in," Azucena says. "I couldn't believe it. It was so mean. But some people just don't like immigrants. They think we are stealing American jobs."

Another problem was Azucena's family. They weren't as close in the U.S. In Peru, they all ate breakfast together. Here, they were too busy. Making money is too important in the United States, she says.

Azucena also worried about her plans for the future. She and her mother did not have enough money to pay for college.

The U.S. government gives **loans** and money to students who need it for college. But these students have to be legal. Or they have to have a green card. A green card means you have permission to live and work in the U.S.

Azucena got her green card in May 2001. Then she could go to college. She wants to become a psychologist.

Azucena **applied** for a green card. Her stepfather was an American **citizen**. She thought she had a good chance.

But then three years passed. She didn't hear from the government.

Azucena became **frustrated**. "I loved school more than any other kid in my class," she said. But she couldn't go.

Finally, she made up another social security number. And she went to a community college. She knew that the college would find out she wasn't legal. And her courses wouldn't count. But she just wanted to be in a classroom. She wanted to learn.

Azucena says, "I want to sit in a classroom with other students and talk about books or science or psychology. That's my American dream."

In 2001, the first part of Azucena's American dream came true. She got her green card. And she signed up for college.

Do you think Azucena will do well at college? Why or why not?

Glossary

alien *(noun)* someone not from the place where they live

applied *(verb)* asked for something

border *(noun)* the edge of a country

citizen *(noun)* a person who has a right to live in a certain country either by birth or by permission

civil war *(noun)* a war between two groups in the same country

Communists *(noun)* people who belong to the Communist political party. They believe that all homes, businesses, and land belong to the government.

community *(noun)* a group of people who live in the same area

confidence *(noun)* a strong belief in oneself

cymbals *(noun)* musical instruments made of brass and shaped like plates

diversity *(noun)* a variety

frustrated *(adjective)* feeling unhappy when something doesn't work out

green card *(noun)* a card that says the U.S. government allows an immigrant to live and work in the U.S.

homeland *(noun)* the place where someone is from

illegal *(adjective)* against the law

immigrants *(noun)* people who leave their country for a new country

karaoke *(noun)* a form of entertainment that started in Japan. People sing while a machine plays music in the background.

Latino *(adjective)* a person who was born in or lives in Latin America; also a person whose family is from Latin America

loans *(noun)* money that someone must pay back

merchant *(noun)* someone who sells things

mosque *(noun)* a building used by Muslims for worship

Muslim *(noun)* a person who follows the religion of Islam

nation *(noun)* a country

poverty *(noun)* the state of being poor

privileges *(noun)* special rights given to a person or group of people

psychologist *(noun)* someone who studies people's minds and emotions

rebels *(noun)* people who fight against the government

refugee *(noun)* a person who is forced to leave his or her home

social security number *(noun)* an ID number the United States government gives to every citizen

volunteer *(noun)* a person who does a job without pay